THIS *journal* BELONGS TO:

A

WEBSITE	
USERNAME	
PASSWORD	
PIN/HINT	
OTHER	

WEBSITE	
USERNAME	
PASSWORD	
PIN/HINT	
OTHER	

WEBSITE	
USERNAME	
PASSWORD	
PIN/HINT	
OTHER	

WEBSITE	
USERNAME	
PASSWORD	
PIN/HINT	
OTHER	

A

WEBSITE	
USERNAME	
PASSWORD	
PIN/HINT	
OTHER	

WEBSITE	
USERNAME	
PASSWORD	
PIN/HINT	
OTHER	

WEBSITE	
USERNAME	
PASSWORD	
PIN/HINT	
OTHER	

WEBSITE	
USERNAME	
PASSWORD	
PIN/HINT	
OTHER	

A

WEBSITE

USERNAME

PASSWORD

PIN/HINT

OTHER

WEBSITE

USERNAME

PASSWORD

PIN/HINT

OTHER

WEBSITE

USERNAME

PASSWORD

PIN/HINT

OTHER

WEBSITE

USERNAME

PASSWORD

PIN/HINT

OTHER

A

WEBSITE	
USERNAME	
PASSWORD	
PIN/HINT	
OTHER	

WEBSITE	
USERNAME	
PASSWORD	
PIN/HINT	
OTHER	

WEBSITE	
USERNAME	
PASSWORD	
PIN/HINT	
OTHER	

WEBSITE	
USERNAME	
PASSWORD	
PIN/HINT	
OTHER	

B

WEBSITE

USERNAME

PASSWORD

PIN/HINT

OTHER

WEBSITE

USERNAME

PASSWORD

PIN/HINT

OTHER

WEBSITE

USERNAME

PASSWORD

PIN/HINT

OTHER

WEBSITE

USERNAME

PASSWORD

PIN/HINT

OTHER

B

WEBSITE	
USERNAME	
PASSWORD	
PIN/HINT	
OTHER	

WEBSITE	
USERNAME	
PASSWORD	
PIN/HINT	
OTHER	

WEBSITE	
USERNAME	
PASSWORD	
PIN/HINT	
OTHER	

WEBSITE	
USERNAME	
PASSWORD	
PIN/HINT	
OTHER	

B

WEBSITE
USERNAME
PASSWORD
PIN/HINT
OTHER

WEBSITE
USERNAME
PASSWORD
PIN/HINT
OTHER

WEBSITE
USERNAME
PASSWORD
PIN/HINT
OTHER

WEBSITE
USERNAME
PASSWORD
PIN/HINT
OTHER

B

WEBSITE

USERNAME

PASSWORD

PIN/HINT

OTHER

WEBSITE

USERNAME

PASSWORD

PIN/HINT

OTHER

WEBSITE

USERNAME

PASSWORD

PIN/HINT

OTHER

WEBSITE

USERNAME

PASSWORD

PIN/HINT

OTHER

WEBSITE

USERNAME

PASSWORD

PIN/HINT

OTHER

WEBSITE

USERNAME

PASSWORD

PIN/HINT

OTHER

WEBSITE

USERNAME

PASSWORD

PIN/HINT

OTHER

WEBSITE

USERNAME

PASSWORD

PIN/HINT

OTHER

WEBSITE	
USERNAME	
PASSWORD	
PIN/HINT	
OTHER	

WEBSITE	
USERNAME	
PASSWORD	
PIN/HINT	
OTHER	

WEBSITE	
USERNAME	
PASSWORD	
PIN/HINT	
OTHER	

WEBSITE	
USERNAME	
PASSWORD	
PIN/HINT	
OTHER	

C

WEBSITE
USERNAME
PASSWORD
PIN/HINT
OTHER

WEBSITE
USERNAME
PASSWORD
PIN/HINT
OTHER

WEBSITE
USERNAME
PASSWORD
PIN/HINT
OTHER

WEBSITE
USERNAME
PASSWORD
PIN/HINT
OTHER

C

WEBSITE	
USERNAME	
PASSWORD	
PIN/HINT	
OTHER	

WEBSITE	
USERNAME	
PASSWORD	
PIN/HINT	
OTHER	

WEBSITE	
USERNAME	
PASSWORD	
PIN/HINT	
OTHER	

WEBSITE	
USERNAME	
PASSWORD	
PIN/HINT	
OTHER	

D

WEBSITE
USERNAME
PASSWORD
PIN/HINT
OTHER

WEBSITE
USERNAME
PASSWORD
PIN/HINT
OTHER

WEBSITE
USERNAME
PASSWORD
PIN/HINT
OTHER

WEBSITE
USERNAME
PASSWORD
PIN/HINT
OTHER

D

WEBSITE	
USERNAME	
PASSWORD	
PIN/HINT	
OTHER	

WEBSITE	
USERNAME	
PASSWORD	
PIN/HINT	
OTHER	

WEBSITE	
USERNAME	
PASSWORD	
PIN/HINT	
OTHER	

WEBSITE	
USERNAME	
PASSWORD	
PIN/HINT	
OTHER	

D

WEBSITE
USERNAME
PASSWORD
PIN/HINT
OTHER

WEBSITE
USERNAME
PASSWORD
PIN/HINT
OTHER

WEBSITE
USERNAME
PASSWORD
PIN/HINT
OTHER

WEBSITE
USERNAME
PASSWORD
PIN/HINT
OTHER

D

WEBSITE

USERNAME

PASSWORD

PIN/HINT

OTHER

WEBSITE

USERNAME

PASSWORD

PIN/HINT

OTHER

WEBSITE

USERNAME

PASSWORD

PIN/HINT

OTHER

WEBSITE

USERNAME

PASSWORD

PIN/HINT

OTHER

E

WEBSITE
USERNAME
PASSWORD
PIN/HINT
OTHER

WEBSITE
USERNAME
PASSWORD
PIN/HINT
OTHER

WEBSITE
USERNAME
PASSWORD
PIN/HINT
OTHER

WEBSITE
USERNAME
PASSWORD
PIN/HINT
OTHER

WEBSITE	
USERNAME	
PASSWORD	
PIN/HINT	
OTHER	

WEBSITE	
USERNAME	
PASSWORD	
PIN/HINT	
OTHER	

WEBSITE	
USERNAME	
PASSWORD	
PIN/HINT	
OTHER	

WEBSITE	
USERNAME	
PASSWORD	
PIN/HINT	
OTHER	

E

WEBSITE
USERNAME
PASSWORD
PIN/HINT
OTHER

WEBSITE
USERNAME
PASSWORD
PIN/HINT
OTHER

WEBSITE
USERNAME
PASSWORD
PIN/HINT
OTHER

WEBSITE
USERNAME
PASSWORD
PIN/HINT
OTHER

WEBSITE	
USERNAME	
PASSWORD	
PIN/HINT	
OTHER	

WEBSITE	
USERNAME	
PASSWORD	
PIN/HINT	
OTHER	

WEBSITE	
USERNAME	
PASSWORD	
PIN/HINT	
OTHER	

WEBSITE	
USERNAME	
PASSWORD	
PIN/HINT	
OTHER	

F

WEBSITE

USERNAME

PASSWORD

PIN/HINT

OTHER

WEBSITE

USERNAME

PASSWORD

PIN/HINT

OTHER

WEBSITE

USERNAME

PASSWORD

PIN/HINT

OTHER

WEBSITE

USERNAME

PASSWORD

PIN/HINT

OTHER

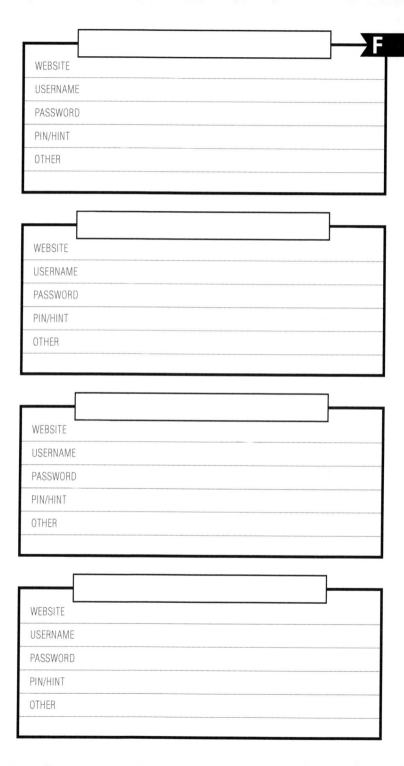

F

WEBSITE

USERNAME

PASSWORD

PIN/HINT

OTHER

WEBSITE

USERNAME

PASSWORD

PIN/HINT

OTHER

WEBSITE

USERNAME

PASSWORD

PIN/HINT

OTHER

WEBSITE

USERNAME

PASSWORD

PIN/HINT

OTHER

F

WEBSITE

USERNAME

PASSWORD

PIN/HINT

OTHER

WEBSITE

USERNAME

PASSWORD

PIN/HINT

OTHER

WEBSITE

USERNAME

PASSWORD

PIN/HINT

OTHER

WEBSITE

USERNAME

PASSWORD

PIN/HINT

OTHER

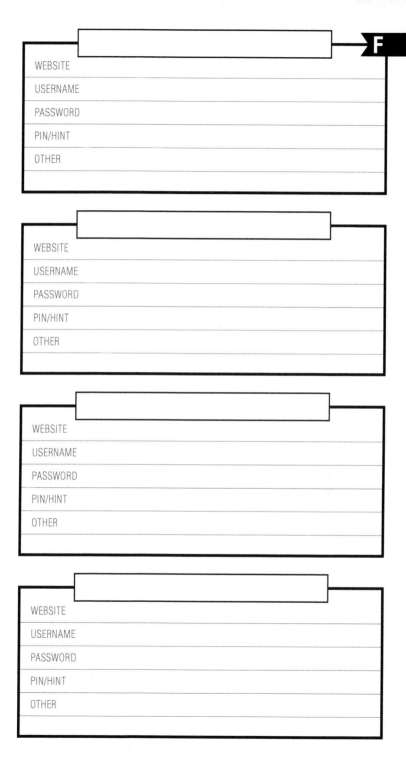

F

WEBSITE

USERNAME

PASSWORD

PIN/HINT

OTHER

WEBSITE

USERNAME

PASSWORD

PIN/HINT

OTHER

WEBSITE

USERNAME

PASSWORD

PIN/HINT

OTHER

WEBSITE

USERNAME

PASSWORD

PIN/HINT

OTHER

WEBSITE	
USERNAME	
PASSWORD	
PIN/HINT	
OTHER	

WEBSITE	
USERNAME	
PASSWORD	
PIN/HINT	
OTHER	

WEBSITE	
USERNAME	
PASSWORD	
PIN/HINT	
OTHER	

WEBSITE	
USERNAME	
PASSWORD	
PIN/HINT	
OTHER	

WEBSITE	
USERNAME	
PASSWORD	
PIN/HINT	
OTHER	

WEBSITE	
USERNAME	
PASSWORD	
PIN/HINT	
OTHER	

WEBSITE	
USERNAME	
PASSWORD	
PIN/HINT	
OTHER	

WEBSITE	
USERNAME	
PASSWORD	
PIN/HINT	
OTHER	

G

WEBSITE	
USERNAME	
PASSWORD	
PIN/HINT	
OTHER	

WEBSITE	
USERNAME	
PASSWORD	
PIN/HINT	
OTHER	

WEBSITE	
USERNAME	
PASSWORD	
PIN/HINT	
OTHER	

WEBSITE	
USERNAME	
PASSWORD	
PIN/HINT	
OTHER	

WEBSITE	
USERNAME	
PASSWORD	
PIN/HINT	
OTHER	

WEBSITE	
USERNAME	
PASSWORD	
PIN/HINT	
OTHER	

WEBSITE	
USERNAME	
PASSWORD	
PIN/HINT	
OTHER	

WEBSITE	
USERNAME	
PASSWORD	
PIN/HINT	
OTHER	

H

WEBSITE

USERNAME

PASSWORD

PIN/HINT

OTHER

WEBSITE

USERNAME

PASSWORD

PIN/HINT

OTHER

WEBSITE

USERNAME

PASSWORD

PIN/HINT

OTHER

WEBSITE

USERNAME

PASSWORD

PIN/HINT

OTHER

WEBSITE

USERNAME

PASSWORD

PIN/HINT

OTHER

WEBSITE

USERNAME

PASSWORD

PIN/HINT

OTHER

WEBSITE

USERNAME

PASSWORD

PIN/HINT

OTHER

WEBSITE

USERNAME

PASSWORD

PIN/HINT

OTHER

H

WEBSITE

USERNAME

PASSWORD

PIN/HINT

OTHER

WEBSITE

USERNAME

PASSWORD

PIN/HINT

OTHER

WEBSITE

USERNAME

PASSWORD

PIN/HINT

OTHER

WEBSITE

USERNAME

PASSWORD

PIN/HINT

OTHER

WEBSITE	
USERNAME	
PASSWORD	
PIN/HINT	
OTHER	

WEBSITE	
USERNAME	
PASSWORD	
PIN/HINT	
OTHER	

WEBSITE	
USERNAME	
PASSWORD	
PIN/HINT	
OTHER	

WEBSITE	
USERNAME	
PASSWORD	
PIN/HINT	
OTHER	

WEBSITE

USERNAME

PASSWORD

PIN/HINT

OTHER

WEBSITE

USERNAME

PASSWORD

PIN/HINT

OTHER

WEBSITE

USERNAME

PASSWORD

PIN/HINT

OTHER

WEBSITE

USERNAME

PASSWORD

PIN/HINT

OTHER

WEBSITE

USERNAME

PASSWORD

PIN/HINT

OTHER

WEBSITE

USERNAME

PASSWORD

PIN/HINT

OTHER

WEBSITE

USERNAME

PASSWORD

PIN/HINT

OTHER

WEBSITE

USERNAME

PASSWORD

PIN/HINT

OTHER

WEBSITE

USERNAME

PASSWORD

PIN/HINT

OTHER

WEBSITE

USERNAME

PASSWORD

PIN/HINT

OTHER

WEBSITE

USERNAME

PASSWORD

PIN/HINT

OTHER

WEBSITE

USERNAME

PASSWORD

PIN/HINT

OTHER

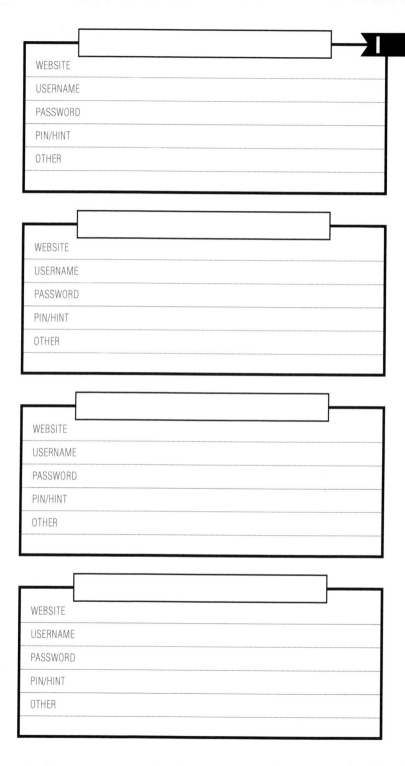

WEBSITE

USERNAME

PASSWORD

PIN/HINT

OTHER

WEBSITE

USERNAME

PASSWORD

PIN/HINT

OTHER

WEBSITE

USERNAME

PASSWORD

PIN/HINT

OTHER

WEBSITE

USERNAME

PASSWORD

PIN/HINT

OTHER

J

WEBSITE	
USERNAME	
PASSWORD	
PIN/HINT	
OTHER	

WEBSITE	
USERNAME	
PASSWORD	
PIN/HINT	
OTHER	

WEBSITE	
USERNAME	
PASSWORD	
PIN/HINT	
OTHER	

WEBSITE	
USERNAME	
PASSWORD	
PIN/HINT	
OTHER	

WEBSITE	
USERNAME	
PASSWORD	
PIN/HINT	
OTHER	

WEBSITE	
USERNAME	
PASSWORD	
PIN/HINT	
OTHER	

WEBSITE	
USERNAME	
PASSWORD	
PIN/HINT	
OTHER	

WEBSITE	
USERNAME	
PASSWORD	
PIN/HINT	
OTHER	

J

WEBSITE	
USERNAME	
PASSWORD	
PIN/HINT	
OTHER	

WEBSITE	
USERNAME	
PASSWORD	
PIN/HINT	
OTHER	

WEBSITE	
USERNAME	
PASSWORD	
PIN/HINT	
OTHER	

WEBSITE	
USERNAME	
PASSWORD	
PIN/HINT	
OTHER	

WEBSITE	
USERNAME	
PASSWORD	
PIN/HINT	
OTHER	

WEBSITE	
USERNAME	
PASSWORD	
PIN/HINT	
OTHER	

WEBSITE	
USERNAME	
PASSWORD	
PIN/HINT	
OTHER	

WEBSITE	
USERNAME	
PASSWORD	
PIN/HINT	
OTHER	

K

WEBSITE

USERNAME

PASSWORD

PIN/HINT

OTHER

WEBSITE

USERNAME

PASSWORD

PIN/HINT

OTHER

WEBSITE

USERNAME

PASSWORD

PIN/HINT

OTHER

WEBSITE

USERNAME

PASSWORD

PIN/HINT

OTHER

K

WEBSITE	
USERNAME	
PASSWORD	
PIN/HINT	
OTHER	

WEBSITE	
USERNAME	
PASSWORD	
PIN/HINT	
OTHER	

WEBSITE	
USERNAME	
PASSWORD	
PIN/HINT	
OTHER	

WEBSITE	
USERNAME	
PASSWORD	
PIN/HINT	
OTHER	

K

WEBSITE
USERNAME
PASSWORD
PIN/HINT
OTHER

WEBSITE
USERNAME
PASSWORD
PIN/HINT
OTHER

WEBSITE
USERNAME
PASSWORD
PIN/HINT
OTHER

WEBSITE
USERNAME
PASSWORD
PIN/HINT
OTHER

K

WEBSITE	
USERNAME	
PASSWORD	
PIN/HINT	
OTHER	

WEBSITE	
USERNAME	
PASSWORD	
PIN/HINT	
OTHER	

WEBSITE	
USERNAME	
PASSWORD	
PIN/HINT	
OTHER	

WEBSITE	
USERNAME	
PASSWORD	
PIN/HINT	
OTHER	

L

WEBSITE	
USERNAME	
PASSWORD	
PIN/HINT	
OTHER	

WEBSITE	
USERNAME	
PASSWORD	
PIN/HINT	
OTHER	

WEBSITE	
USERNAME	
PASSWORD	
PIN/HINT	
OTHER	

WEBSITE	
USERNAME	
PASSWORD	
PIN/HINT	
OTHER	

L

WEBSITE	
USERNAME	
PASSWORD	
PIN/HINT	
OTHER	

WEBSITE	
USERNAME	
PASSWORD	
PIN/HINT	
OTHER	

WEBSITE	
USERNAME	
PASSWORD	
PIN/HINT	
OTHER	

WEBSITE	
USERNAME	
PASSWORD	
PIN/HINT	
OTHER	

L

WEBSITE

USERNAME

PASSWORD

PIN/HINT

OTHER

WEBSITE

USERNAME

PASSWORD

PIN/HINT

OTHER

WEBSITE

USERNAME

PASSWORD

PIN/HINT

OTHER

WEBSITE

USERNAME

PASSWORD

PIN/HINT

OTHER

WEBSITE

USERNAME

PASSWORD

PIN/HINT

OTHER

WEBSITE

USERNAME

PASSWORD

PIN/HINT

OTHER

WEBSITE

USERNAME

PASSWORD

PIN/HINT

OTHER

WEBSITE

USERNAME

PASSWORD

PIN/HINT

OTHER

M

WEBSITE	
USERNAME	
PASSWORD	
PIN/HINT	
OTHER	

WEBSITE	
USERNAME	
PASSWORD	
PIN/HINT	
OTHER	

WEBSITE	
USERNAME	
PASSWORD	
PIN/HINT	
OTHER	

WEBSITE	
USERNAME	
PASSWORD	
PIN/HINT	
OTHER	

WEBSITE
USERNAME
PASSWORD
PIN/HINT
OTHER

WEBSITE
USERNAME
PASSWORD
PIN/HINT
OTHER

WEBSITE
USERNAME
PASSWORD
PIN/HINT
OTHER

WEBSITE
USERNAME
PASSWORD
PIN/HINT
OTHER

M

WEBSITE

USERNAME

PASSWORD

PIN/HINT

OTHER

WEBSITE

USERNAME

PASSWORD

PIN/HINT

OTHER

WEBSITE

USERNAME

PASSWORD

PIN/HINT

OTHER

WEBSITE

USERNAME

PASSWORD

PIN/HINT

OTHER

M

WEBSITE	
USERNAME	
PASSWORD	
PIN/HINT	
OTHER	

WEBSITE	
USERNAME	
PASSWORD	
PIN/HINT	
OTHER	

WEBSITE	
USERNAME	
PASSWORD	
PIN/HINT	
OTHER	

WEBSITE	
USERNAME	
PASSWORD	
PIN/HINT	
OTHER	

N

WEBSITE	
USERNAME	
PASSWORD	
PIN/HINT	
OTHER	

WEBSITE	
USERNAME	
PASSWORD	
PIN/HINT	
OTHER	

WEBSITE	
USERNAME	
PASSWORD	
PIN/HINT	
OTHER	

WEBSITE	
USERNAME	
PASSWORD	
PIN/HINT	
OTHER	

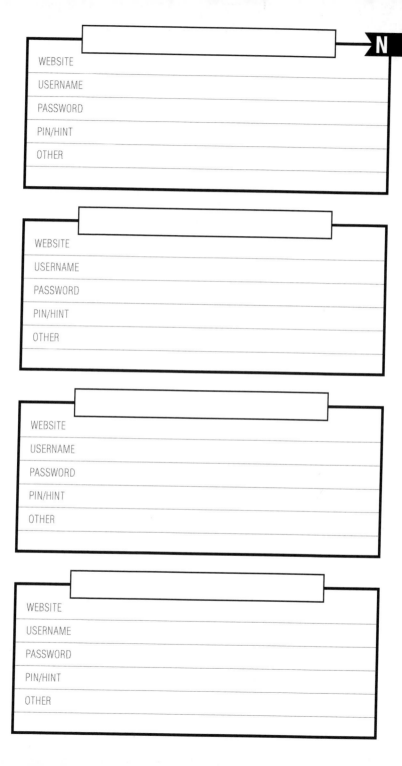

WEBSITE

USERNAME

PASSWORD

PIN/HINT

OTHER

WEBSITE

USERNAME

PASSWORD

PIN/HINT

OTHER

WEBSITE

USERNAME

PASSWORD

PIN/HINT

OTHER

WEBSITE

USERNAME

PASSWORD

PIN/HINT

OTHER

N

WEBSITE	
USERNAME	
PASSWORD	
PIN/HINT	
OTHER	

WEBSITE	
USERNAME	
PASSWORD	
PIN/HINT	
OTHER	

WEBSITE	
USERNAME	
PASSWORD	
PIN/HINT	
OTHER	

WEBSITE	
USERNAME	
PASSWORD	
PIN/HINT	
OTHER	

WEBSITE	
USERNAME	
PASSWORD	
PIN/HINT	
OTHER	

WEBSITE	
USERNAME	
PASSWORD	
PIN/HINT	
OTHER	

WEBSITE	
USERNAME	
PASSWORD	
PIN/HINT	
OTHER	

WEBSITE	
USERNAME	
PASSWORD	
PIN/HINT	
OTHER	

0

WEBSITE

USERNAME

PASSWORD

PIN/HINT

OTHER

WEBSITE

USERNAME

PASSWORD

PIN/HINT

OTHER

WFRSITE

USERNAME

PASSWORD

PIN/HINT

OTHER

WEBSITE

USERNAME

PASSWORD

PIN/HINT

OTHER

0

WEBSITE

USERNAME

PASSWORD

PIN/HINT

OTHER

WEBSITE

USERNAME

PASSWORD

PIN/HINT

OTHER

WEBSITE

USERNAME

PASSWORD

PIN/HINT

OTHER

WEBSITE

USERNAME

PASSWORD

PIN/HINT

OTHER

0

WEBSITE

USERNAME

PASSWORD

PIN/HINT

OTHER

WEBSITE

USERNAME

PASSWORD

PIN/HINT

OTHER

WEBSITE

USERNAME

PASSWORD

PIN/HINT

OTHER

WEBSITE

USERNAME

PASSWORD

PIN/HINT

OTHER

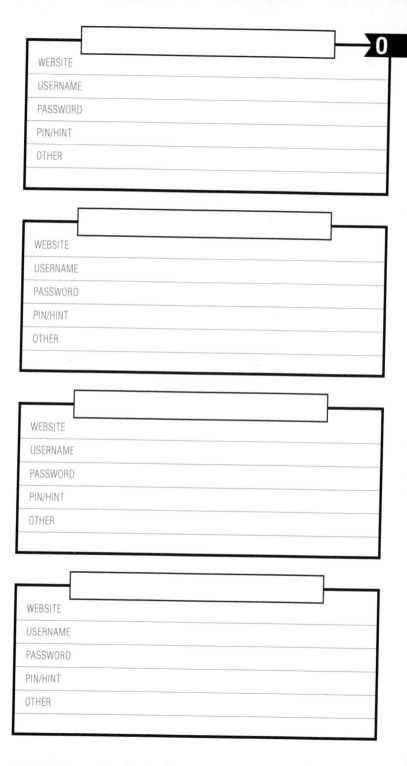

0

WEBSITE

USERNAME

PASSWORD

PIN/HINT

OTHER

WEBSITE

USERNAME

PASSWORD

PIN/HINT

OTHER

WEBSITE

USERNAME

PASSWORD

PIN/HINT

OTHER

WEBSITE

USERNAME

PASSWORD

PIN/HINT

OTHER

P

WEBSITE

USERNAME

PASSWORD

PIN/HINT

OTHER

WEBSITE

USERNAME

PASSWORD

PIN/HINT

OTHER

WEBSITE

USERNAME

PASSWORD

PIN/HINT

OTHER

WEBSITE

USERNAME

PASSWORD

PIN/HINT

OTHER

WEBSITE

USERNAME

PASSWORD

PIN/HINT

OTHER

WEBSITE

USERNAME

PASSWORD

PIN/HINT

OTHER

WEBSITE

USERNAME

PASSWORD

PIN/HINT

OTHER

WEBSITE

USERNAME

PASSWORD

PIN/HINT

OTHER

P

WEBSITE
USERNAME
PASSWORD
PIN/HINT
OTHER

WEBSITE
USERNAME
PASSWORD
PIN/HINT
OTHER

WEBSITE
USERNAME
PASSWORD
PIN/HINT
OTHER

WEBSITE
USERNAME
PASSWORD
PIN/HINT
OTHER

WEBSITE	
USERNAME	
PASSWORD	
PIN/HINT	
OTHER	

WEBSITE	
USERNAME	
PASSWORD	
PIN/HINT	
OTHER	

WEBSITE	
USERNAME	
PASSWORD	
PIN/HINT	
OTHER	

WEBSITE	
USERNAME	
PASSWORD	
PIN/HINT	
OTHER	

Q

WEBSITE	
USERNAME	
PASSWORD	
PIN/HINT	
OTHER	

WEBSITE	
USERNAME	
PASSWORD	
PIN/HINT	
OTHER	

WEBSITE	
USERNAME	
PASSWORD	
PIN/HINT	
OTHER	

WEBSITE	
USERNAME	
PASSWORD	
PIN/HINT	
OTHER	

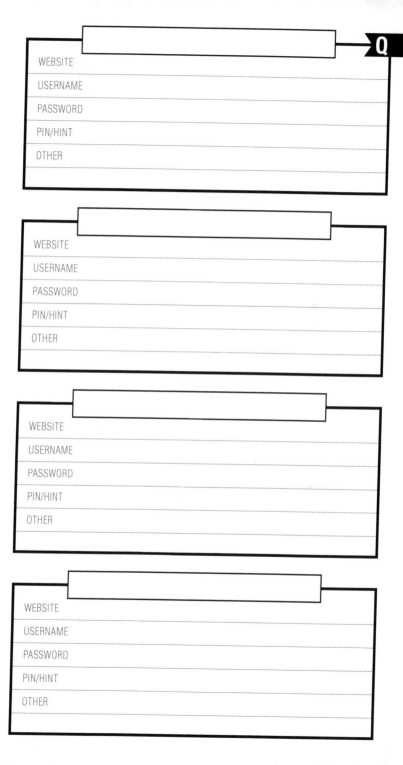

Q

WEBSITE

USERNAME

PASSWORD

PIN/HINT

OTHER

WEBSITE

USERNAME

PASSWORD

PIN/HINT

OTHER

WEBSITE

USERNAME

PASSWORD

PIN/HINT

OTHER

WEBSITE

USERNAME

PASSWORD

PIN/HINT

OTHER

Q

WEBSITE

USERNAME

PASSWORD

PIN/HINT

OTHER

WEBSITE

USERNAME

PASSWORD

PIN/HINT

OTHER

WEBSITE

USERNAME

PASSWORD

PIN/HINT

OTHER

WEBSITE

USERNAME

PASSWORD

PIN/HINT

OTHER

Q

WEBSITE	
USERNAME	
PASSWORD	
PIN/HINT	
OTHER	

WEBSITE	
USERNAME	
PASSWORD	
PIN/HINT	
OTHER	

WEBSITE	
USERNAME	
PASSWORD	
PIN/HINT	
OTHER	

WEBSITE	
USERNAME	
PASSWORD	
PIN/HINT	
OTHER	

R

WEBSITE	
USERNAME	
PASSWORD	
PIN/HINT	
OTHER	

WEBSITE	
USERNAME	
PASSWORD	
PIN/HINT	
OTHER	

WEBSITE	
USERNAME	
PASSWORD	
PIN/HINT	
OTHER	

WEBSITE	
USERNAME	
PASSWORD	
PIN/HINT	
OTHER	

R

WEBSITE

USERNAME

PASSWORD

PIN/HINT

OTHER

WEBSITE

USERNAME

PASSWORD

PIN/HINT

OTHER

WEBSITE

USERNAME

PASSWORD

PIN/HINT

OTHER

WEBSITE

USERNAME

PASSWORD

PIN/HINT

OTHER

R

WEBSITE

USERNAME

PASSWORD

PIN/HINT

OTHER

WEBSITE

USERNAME

PASSWORD

PIN/HINT

OTHER

WEBSITE

USERNAME

PASSWORD

PIN/HINT

OTHER

WEBSITE

USERNAME

PASSWORD

PIN/HINT

OTHER

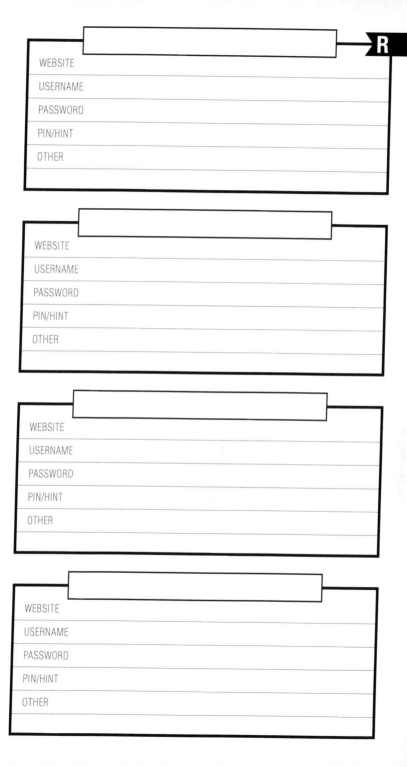

R

WEBSITE	
USERNAME	
PASSWORD	
PIN/HINT	
OTHER	

WEBSITE	
USERNAME	
PASSWORD	
PIN/HINT	
OTHER	

WEBSITE	
USERNAME	
PASSWORD	
PIN/HINT	
OTHER	

WEBSITE	
USERNAME	
PASSWORD	
PIN/HINT	
OTHER	

S

WEBSITE	
USERNAME	
PASSWORD	
PIN/HINT	
OTHER	

WEBSITE	
USERNAME	
PASSWORD	
PIN/HINT	
OTHER	

WEBSITE	
USERNAME	
PASSWORD	
PIN/HINT	
OTHER	

WEBSITE	
USERNAME	
PASSWORD	
PIN/HINT	
OTHER	

S

WEBSITE

USERNAME

PASSWORD

PIN/HINT

OTHER

WEBSITE

USERNAME

PASSWORD

PIN/HINT

OTHER

WEBSITE

USERNAME

PASSWORD

PIN/HINT

OTHER

WEBSITE

USERNAME

PASSWORD

PIN/HINT

OTHER

S

WEBSITE

USERNAME

PASSWORD

PIN/HINT

OTHER

WEBSITE

USERNAME

PASSWORD

PIN/HINT

OTHER

WEBSITE

USERNAME

PASSWORD

PIN/HINT

OTHER

WEBSITE

USERNAME

PASSWORD

PIN/HINT

OTHER

S

WEBSITE	
USERNAME	
PASSWORD	
PIN/HINT	
OTHER	

WEBSITE	
USERNAME	
PASSWORD	
PIN/HINT	
OTHER	

WEBSITE	
USERNAME	
PASSWORD	
PIN/HINT	
OTHER	

WEBSITE	
USERNAME	
PASSWORD	
PIN/HINT	
OTHER	

T

WEBSITE	
USERNAME	
PASSWORD	
PIN/HINT	
OTHER	

WEBSITE	
USERNAME	
PASSWORD	
PIN/HINT	
OTHER	

WEBSITE	
USERNAME	
PASSWORD	
PIN/HINT	
OTHER	

WEBSITE	
USERNAME	
PASSWORD	
PIN/HINT	
OTHER	

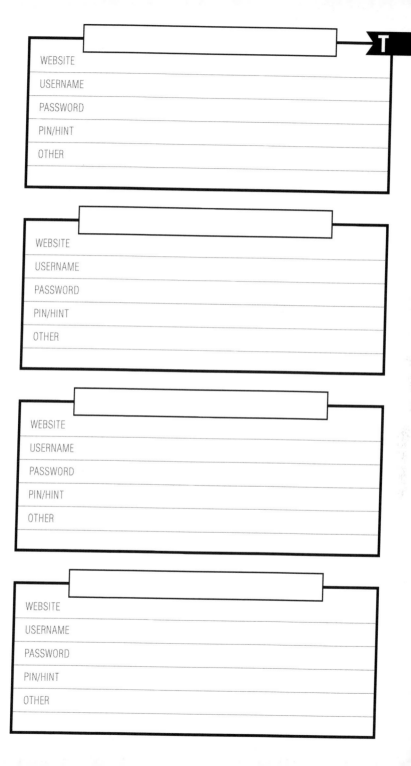

T

WEBSITE

USERNAME

PASSWORD

PIN/HINT

OTHER

WEBSITE

USERNAME

PASSWORD

PIN/HINT

OTHER

WEBSITE

USERNAME

PASSWORD

PIN/HINT

OTHER

WEBSITE

USERNAME

PASSWORD

PIN/HINT

OTHER

T

WEBSITE	
USERNAME	
PASSWORD	
PIN/HINT	
OTHER	

WEBSITE	
USERNAME	
PASSWORD	
PIN/HINT	
OTHER	

WEBSITE	
USERNAME	
PASSWORD	
PIN/HINT	
OTHER	

WEBSITE	
USERNAME	
PASSWORD	
PIN/HINT	
OTHER	

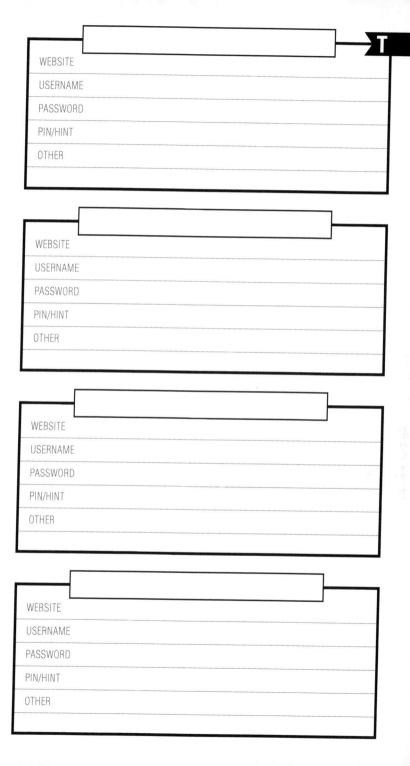

T

WEBSITE

USERNAME

PASSWORD

PIN/HINT

OTHER

WEBSITE

USERNAME

PASSWORD

PIN/HINT

OTHER

WEBSITE

USERNAME

PASSWORD

PIN/HINT

OTHER

WEBSITE

USERNAME

PASSWORD

PIN/HINT

OTHER

U

WEBSITE

USERNAME

PASSWORD

PIN/HINT

OTHER

WEBSITE

USERNAME

PASSWORD

PIN/HINT

OTHER

WFRSITE

USERNAME

PASSWORD

PIN/HINT

OTHER

WEBSITE

USERNAME

PASSWORD

PIN/HINT

OTHER

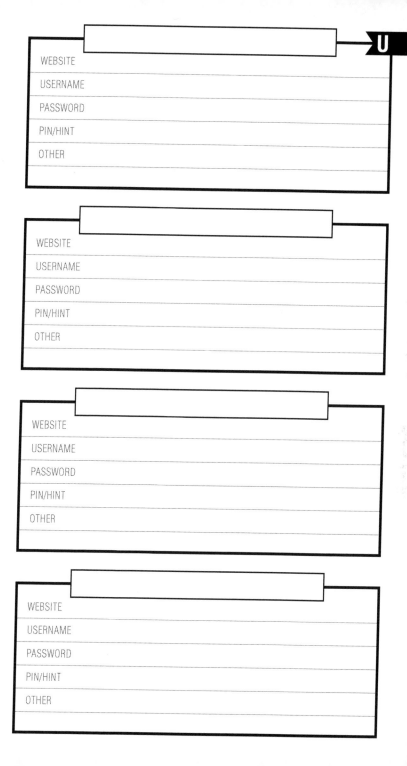

U

WEBSITE	
USERNAME	
PASSWORD	
PIN/HINT	
OTHER	

WEBSITE	
USERNAME	
PASSWORD	
PIN/HINT	
OTHER	

WEBSITE	
USERNAME	
PASSWORD	
PIN/HINT	
OTHER	

WEBSITE	
USERNAME	
PASSWORD	
PIN/HINT	
OTHER	

U

WEBSITE	
USERNAME	
PASSWORD	
PIN/HINT	
OTHER	

WEBSITE	
USERNAME	
PASSWORD	
PIN/HINT	
OTHER	

WEBSITE	
USERNAME	
PASSWORD	
PIN/HINT	
OTHER	

WEBSITE	
USERNAME	
PASSWORD	
PIN/HINT	
OTHER	

U

WEBSITE	
USERNAME	
PASSWORD	
PIN/HINT	
OTHER	

WEBSITE	
USERNAME	
PASSWORD	
PIN/HINT	
OTHER	

WEBSITE	
USERNAME	
PASSWORD	
PIN/HINT	
OTHER	

WEBSITE	
USERNAME	
PASSWORD	
PIN/HINT	
OTHER	

V

WEBSITE	
USERNAME	
PASSWORD	
PIN/HINT	
OTHER	

WEBSITE	
USERNAME	
PASSWORD	
PIN/HINT	
OTHER	

WEBSITE	
USERNAME	
PASSWORD	
PIN/HINT	
OTHER	

WEBSITE	
USERNAME	
PASSWORD	
PIN/HINT	
OTHER	

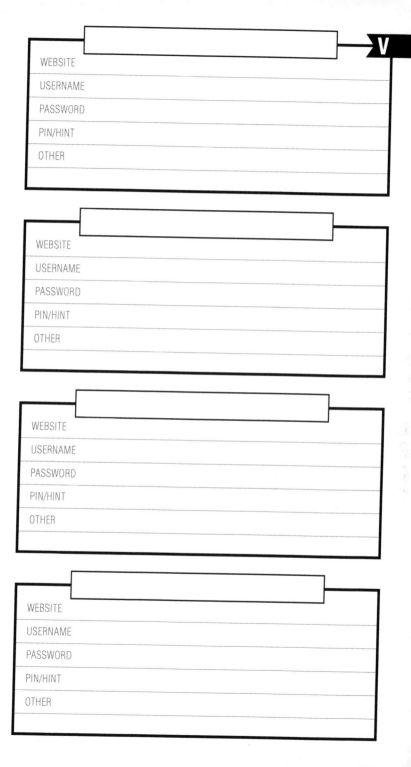

V

WEBSITE

USERNAME

PASSWORD

PIN/HINT

OTHER

WEBSITE

USERNAME

PASSWORD

PIN/HINT

OTHER

WEBSITE

USERNAME

PASSWORD

PIN/HINT

OTHER

WEBSITE

USERNAME

PASSWORD

PIN/HINT

OTHER

WEBSITE

USERNAME

PASSWORD

PIN/HINT

OTHER

WEBSITE

USERNAME

PASSWORD

PIN/HINT

OTHER

WEBSITE

USERNAME

PASSWORD

PIN/HINT

OTHER

WEBSITE

USERNAME

PASSWORD

PIN/HINT

OTHER

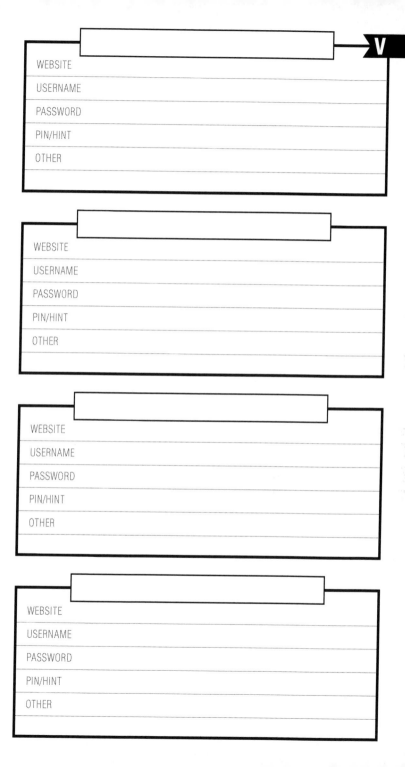

WEBSITE

USERNAME

PASSWORD

PIN/HINT

OTHER

WEBSITE

USERNAME

PASSWORD

PIN/HINT

OTHER

WEBSITE

USERNAME

PASSWORD

PIN/HINT

OTHER

WEBSITE

USERNAME

PASSWORD

PIN/HINT

OTHER

W

WEBSITE	
USERNAME	
PASSWORD	
PIN/HINT	
OTHER	

WEBSITE	
USERNAME	
PASSWORD	
PIN/HINT	
OTHER	

WEBSITE	
USERNAME	
PASSWORD	
PIN/HINT	
OTHER	

WEBSITE	
USERNAME	
PASSWORD	
PIN/HINT	
OTHER	

W

WEBSITE

USERNAME

PASSWORD

PIN/HINT

OTHER

WEBSITE

USERNAME

PASSWORD

PIN/HINT

OTHER

WEBSITE

USERNAME

PASSWORD

PIN/HINT

OTHER

WEBSITE

USERNAME

PASSWORD

PIN/HINT

OTHER

W

WEBSITE

USERNAME

PASSWORD

PIN/HINT

OTHER

WEBSITE

USERNAME

PASSWORD

PIN/HINT

OTHER

WEBSITE

USERNAME

PASSWORD

PIN/HINT

OTHER

WEBSITE

USERNAME

PASSWORD

PIN/HINT

OTHER

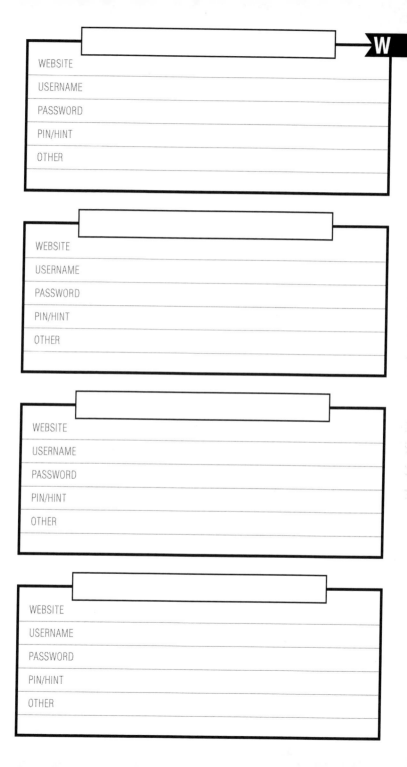

W

WEBSITE

USERNAME

PASSWORD

PIN/HINT

OTHER

WEBSITE

USERNAME

PASSWORD

PIN/HINT

OTHER

WEBSITE

USERNAME

PASSWORD

PIN/HINT

OTHER

WEBSITE

USERNAME

PASSWORD

PIN/HINT

OTHER

X

WEBSITE

USERNAME

PASSWORD

PIN/HINT

OTHER

WEBSITE

USERNAME

PASSWORD

PIN/HINT

OTHER

WEBSITE

USERNAME

PASSWORD

PIN/HINT

OTHER

WEBSITE

USERNAME

PASSWORD

PIN/HINT

OTHER

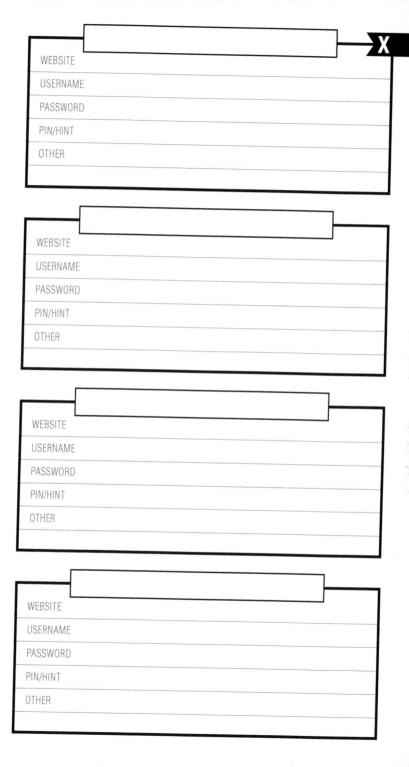

X

WEBSITE	
USERNAME	
PASSWORD	
PIN/HINT	
OTHER	

WEBSITE	
USERNAME	
PASSWORD	
PIN/HINT	
OTHER	

WEBSITE	
USERNAME	
PASSWORD	
PIN/HINT	
OTHER	

WEBSITE	
USERNAME	
PASSWORD	
PIN/HINT	
OTHER	

X

WEBSITE

USERNAME

PASSWORD

PIN/HINT

OTHER

WEBSITE

USERNAME

PASSWORD

PIN/HINT

OTHER

WEBSITE

USERNAME

PASSWORD

PIN/HINT

OTHER

WEBSITE

USERNAME

PASSWORD

PIN/HINT

OTHER

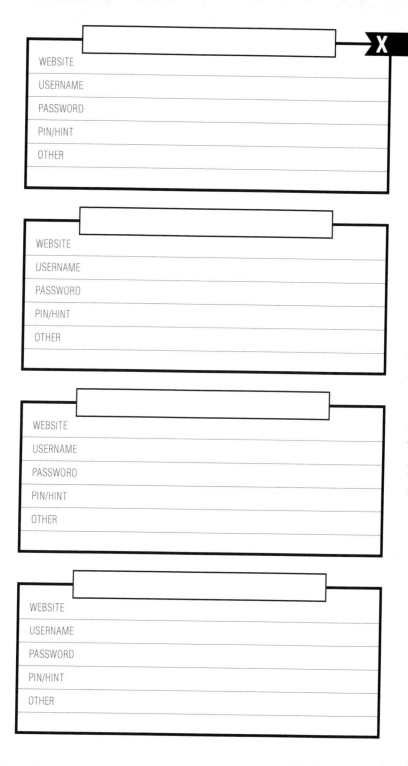

X

WEBSITE

USERNAME

PASSWORD

PIN/HINT

OTHER

WEBSITE

USERNAME

PASSWORD

PIN/HINT

OTHER

WEBSITE

USERNAME

PASSWORD

PIN/HINT

OTHER

WEBSITE

USERNAME

PASSWORD

PIN/HINT

OTHER

Y

WEBSITE

USERNAME

PASSWORD

PIN/HINT

OTHER

WEBSITE

USERNAME

PASSWORD

PIN/HINT

OTHER

WEBSITE

USERNAME

PASSWORD

PIN/HINT

OTHER

WEBSITE

USERNAME

PASSWORD

PIN/HINT

OTHER

Y

WEBSITE

USERNAME

PASSWORD

PIN/HINT

OTHER

WEBSITE

USERNAME

PASSWORD

PIN/HINT

OTHER

WEBSITE

USERNAME

PASSWORD

PIN/HINT

OTHER

WEBSITE

USERNAME

PASSWORD

PIN/HINT

OTHER

WEBSITE

USERNAME

PASSWORD

PIN/HINT

OTHER

WEBSITE

USERNAME

PASSWORD

PIN/HINT

OTHER

WEBSITE

USERNAME

PASSWORD

PIN/HINT

OTHER

WEBSITE

USERNAME

PASSWORD

PIN/HINT

OTHER

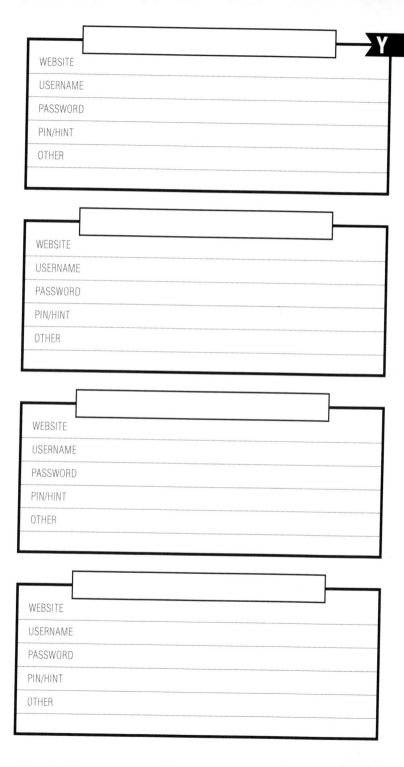

Y

WEBSITE

USERNAME

PASSWORD

PIN/HINT

OTHER

WEBSITE

USERNAME

PASSWORD

PIN/HINT

OTHER

WEBSITE

USERNAME

PASSWORD

PIN/HINT

OTHER

WEBSITE

USERNAME

PASSWORD

PIN/HINT

OTHER

Z

WEBSITE
USERNAME
PASSWORD
PIN/HINT
OTHER

WEBSITE
USERNAME
PASSWORD
PIN/HINT
OTHER

WEBSITE
USERNAME
PASSWORD
PIN/HINT
OTHER

WEBSITE
USERNAME
PASSWORD
PIN/HINT
OTHER

Z

WEBSITE

USERNAME

PASSWORD

PIN/HINT

OTHER

WEBSITE

USERNAME

PASSWORD

PIN/HINT

OTHER

WEBSITE

USERNAME

PASSWORD

PIN/HINT

OTHER

WEBSITE

USERNAME

PASSWORD

PIN/HINT

OTHER

Z

WEBSITE	
USERNAME	
PASSWORD	
PIN/HINT	
OTHER	

WEBSITE	
USERNAME	
PASSWORD	
PIN/HINT	
OTHER	

WEBSITE	
USERNAME	
PASSWORD	
PIN/HINT	
OTHER	

WEBSITE	
USERNAME	
PASSWORD	
PIN/HINT	
OTHER	

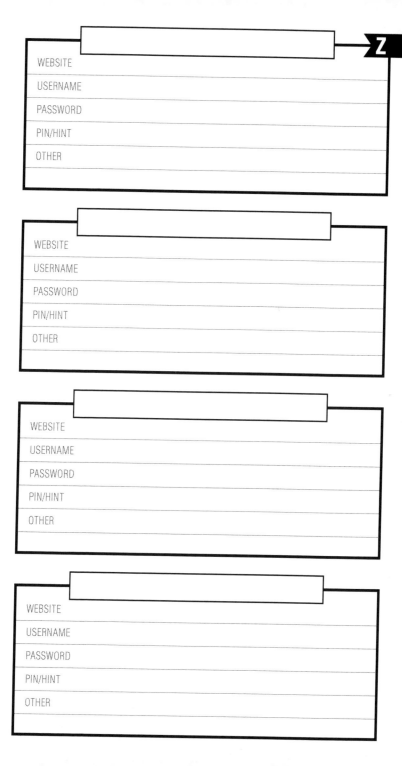

Z

WEBSITE	
USERNAME	
PASSWORD	
PIN/HINT	
OTHER	

WEBSITE	
USERNAME	
PASSWORD	
PIN/HINT	
OTHER	

WEBSITE	
USERNAME	
PASSWORD	
PIN/HINT	
OTHER	

WEBSITE	
USERNAME	
PASSWORD	
PIN/HINT	
OTHER	

Made in the USA
Lexington, KY
08 December 2017